APOCKETFUL
OFBARS

Edited by Melina Deliyannis

A POCKETFUL OF BARS

images
Publishing

Published in Australia in 2006 by
The Images Publishing Group Pty Ltd
ABN 89 059 734 431
6 Bastow Place, Mulgrave, Victoria 3170, Australia
Tel: +61 3 9561 5544 Fax: +61 3 9561 4860
books@images.com.au
www.imagespublishing.com

National Library of Australia Cataloguing-in-Publication entry:

A pocketful of bars.

ISBN 9781864702286.

ISBN 1 86470 228 1

1. Bars (Drinking establishments). I. Deliyannis, Melina.

647.95

Edited by Melina Deliyannis

Designed by The Graphic Image Studio Pty Ltd, Mulgrave, Australia
www.tgis.com.au

Digital production and print by Everbest Printing Co Ltd. in Hong Kong/China

IMAGES has included on its website a page for special notices in relation
to this and our other publications. Please visit www.imagespublishing.com

Contents

Contents

PROJECTS

Afterglow Lounge

EVOKE INTERNATIONAL DESIGN

Afterglow Lounge was conceived as an extension of Glowbal Satay Bar & Grill (a previous Evoke International Design project) and acts as a multifunction space accommodating 30–40 people for cocktails as well as working as an overflow space for the adjoining restaurant

The street-level windows have been covered with a graphic design to create a sensual interpretation of the Afterglow theme, and a sense of privacy for those inside. Small Corian cocktail tables were custom-designed by Evoke and the couches were designed by Bombast Furniture.

The color scheme is hot pink, red, and chocolate brown. The quality of light was an important element of the design so all of the interior walls were painted white, allowing for the glow of the pink lighting to provide a sophisticated and sensual atmosphere.

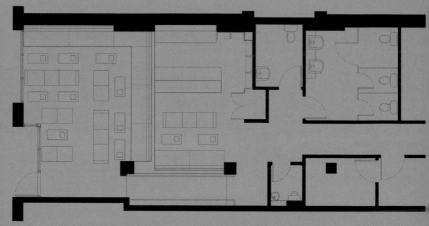

Floor plan

Apollo Bar

DAVID LING ARCHITECT

The German version of the *David Letterman Show* has found its home in two 1950's movie theaters on the Ring Street in Cologne's medieval inner core. Conceived as a TV production studio with multiple uses, the facilities include the actual theater renovation, an exclusive late-night bar run in conjunction with the show, and a comedy club in the cellar. The Late Night Bar is an exclusive enclave specifically for Harald Schmidt and his talk show guests, as well as members of the audience, to commune in a more intimate setting and enjoy a post-show drink.

A curved wall contains the actual bar. Resembling the inside of a ship's hull, it is a curved and sloped cherry wood surface. Opposite this is a lead-clad folded wall. The forms are juxtaposed in a dialectical relationship of opposites: a gentle fetus-shaped curve versus a lightning bolt; the sensual and warm versus hard-edged and metallic.

The bar accommodates up to 100 people and is conceived as a living room of sorts with lounge seating in the form of banquettes and armchairs. The lighting is entirely indirect with the exception of the TV monitors embedded in the walls and niches, and the myriad candles on each table.

hotography: Helmut Stahl

Armani Café

GABELLINI ASSOCIATES

The Armani Café was developed as part of the 100,000-square-foot Armani Center in Milan and opened in October 2000. Gabellini Associates designed the haute vegetarian cuisine restaurant in close collaboration with Giorgio Armani and the restaurant operator. The café required a casual bar space for coffee service and light lunches, as well as a more formal 80-seat dining area.

The café occupies a two-level space on the corner of Via dei Giardini and Via Croce Rossa on an important public plaza, enjoying high visibility and urban views through a full-height glass storefront. The main entrance to the café from the plaza opens into a double-height atrium space that connects the ground-level bar area to the first-level restaurant suspended above. A long stainless steel bar with a floating curved glass counter extends between the atrium bar space and a more intimate seating area below the suspended floor above. A backlit translucent glass corner invites the customer to a walnut staircase winding discreetly around a soft blue corner element to the restaurant area above.

Three sides of the restaurant seating area are wrapped by sliding blue and white acrylic translucent panels that form a horizontal light band around the space. Transverse light slots in the ceiling accentuate the sleek horizontality of the space, projecting views toward the atrium space and the public plaza beyond. The double-height atrium wall pierces the restaurant level, dematerializing at its edge to allow views into an open kitchen through a suspended clear glass corner. An American walnut bench with flexible cushions provides perimeter seating, while custom-carved Corian café tables with elegantly curved bases appear to spring from the poured concrete flooring.

19

Astro Bar

Michael Young Studio was asked to refurbish one of Reykjavik's oldest buildings. Battling with a venue that was protected by heritage laws and a lack of straight lines, a well-designed club with four bars and two dance floors was eventually built.

The architect used the concept of a swimming pool crossed with a picnic area to 'bring in a little bit of the outdoors.' With the assistance of a local pool-building company, the final result is an icy-looking interior redolent of Iceland's weather.

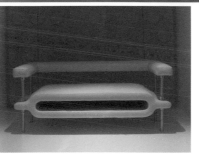

Bambuddha Lounge

NOMADIKA DESIGN STUDIO

The 1950's architecture of this pre-existing building added to the sleek geometry of the new interior. Bambuddha Lounge invites the outdoors in with its large sliding windows that open to the outdoor patio, which features an indoor/outdoor stacked-stone fireplace, and Nipa huts situated around the swimming pool for dining and lounging. The rich, cream-colored, glossy epoxy floor and grass-cloth walls juxtaposed against the dark walnut-stained dining furniture, which is lit from below, give the appearance that the room is levitating. The dining nook with its jewel-toned upholstery, chandeliers, and bronze mirror cut into 10-inch-thick planks resembles a cozy but retro-glamour lounge. The 22-foot walnut-stained bar features mother-of-pearl panels and has five single-stream fountains as its backdrop.

Bar Genf

PLAJER & FRANZ STUDIO

The language and values of the BMW brand were the main influences behind the choice of materials for the walls, floor, and furniture of this sophisticated bar in Geneva. The designers hoped to communicate a sense of comfort and style—concepts synonymous with the dynamic BMW brand. The wood, seat fabric, etched glass, and the use of intelligent materials, such as the wall covering featuring marble gravel in resin, subtly moderate this idea.

Bar IAA

PLAJER & FRANZ STUDIO

The primary intention of a bar space at a trade show is to serve VIPs and the media. A clear overview of the cars presented is as important as the opportunity to rest and meet.

The architects had initially aimed to create a bar with a normal ceiling height, but they were able to use the entire 6 meters to maximize the appearance of the venue and create a strong impression. The space that divides the hanging elements above the bar was used to light the counter and the back. The lamps were installed through a rectangular opening, creating a sharp beam of light on the bar top.

A metal panel behind the bar features printed images of the car design process, while the bar and the floor were built from walnut, creating a mixture of elegant and technical materials, reflecting the dynamism of the BMW brand.

Floor plan

barlounge 808

PLAJER & FRANZ STUDIO

The given theme for barlounge 808 was a 1960's American lounge bar. Its design recalls the cool sophistication of a decade in which patrons made an effort to dress up before sipping Martinis.

The venue is divided into two main areas; a café/bar in the front (serving food and drinks), and a cocktail lounge in the back. Design elements like the aquarium, light coves, and costume furniture determine the relaxed atmosphere in the space. Speakers and air conditioning are invisibly integrated in the wooden wall paneling.

The wedge-shaped venue is situated on a corner. Floor-to-ceiling windows, 40 meters long, front two streets and meet in a glass curve at the street corner. The airy drapes serve a double purpose: they allow those inside to watch the action outside, while projecting seductive glimpses of partying silhouettes to passersby. The windows all open to provide a seamless transition to the terrace so that in summer tables and chairs spill out onto the sidewalk in typical European fashion.

Photography: Fritz Busam

Bear Brass

MADDISON ARCHITECTS

Bear Brass consists of several unique areas within a small tenancy; its size appears to be bigger than it actually is. Spaces were compressed to emphasize tightness and restriction, such as the area in and around the bar. The hydraulic and mechanical service installations were seen as an opportunity to enrich the experience.

The reconfigured and relocated storefront demonstrates ongoing investigations into ways of dissolving the enclosure. This is particularly important, given the connection this tenancy has with the Yarra River promenade and views to the city.

Changes of level in the built-up timber flooring seamlessly flow inside to out, with sliding bi-folding and gas-strutted glass panels disappearing so that the spaces reach toward the city. This gesture is repeated again with the in situ concrete bar tops that flow through the external glazing system.

Photography: Trevor Mein

Bond Lounge Bar

PLAYGROUND MELBOURNE PTY LTD

As a visual creation, Bond draws its influences from a combination of Art Deco ideology and minimalism. The simple concept signifies the design affair with repetition, perspective, and unity, while the emphasis on structural integrity accompanied by diverse surfaces creates softness and warmth. Materials such as hard wood, leather, and multi-faceted tiles initiate style and comfort, and reflect the essence of touch and color reminiscent of the Art Deco era. The use of rare veneers stained in classic Tuscan, mixed with plush carpet and stone, further embodies intimacy and elegance.

Entering the space into the reception area, an inviting mood is set through the use of mixed materials enhanced by a lighting source. Stepping down into the main area, the concave interior that spans from end to end nestles inside the old office space like a cocoon.

The concave ceiling is functional as well as aesthetically pleasing, and creates a depth and perspective that encompasses a great acoustic presence. Sound installations are predominantly hidden in the walls and the room allows for a small live music ensemble to perform in a low-reverberant atmosphere. Video projector and audio ports placed strategically over the entire area allow for multimedia functionality.

Photography: Shania Shegedyn

Borough

BEN KELLY DESIGN

A former warehouse was converted into an extensive bar and restaurant with a members' bar and nine guest rooms. The visitor arrives on a black terrazzo floor that forms a 'runway' from the reception, parallel to the main bar, providing a direct route to the restaurant. The main bar consists of a rough-sawn granite front with polished grooves and a clean polished top, while the rear bar consists of a full-height mirror, tiered glass shelves, and a dramatic display of backlit bottles. The bar is further defined within the space by a pressed-metal ceiling imported from the US and a row of over-scaled globe light fittings

A Douglas fir downstand linking the reception area wraps around the lounge bar at a high level, terminating in a dramatic staircase that leads to the upper level members' bar and rooms. The downstand visually contains the lounge, while providing a servicing barrier and allowing the full ceiling height to be used. Exposed structural beams and clusters of smaller globe fittings dramatize this height.

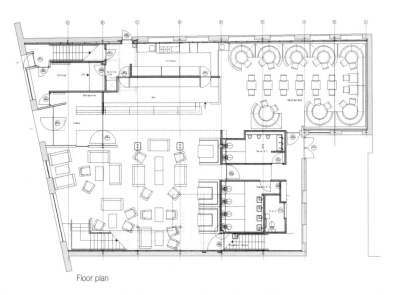

Floor plan

The lounge bar provides seating for 80 on a combination of luxuriously upholstered leather wing chairs, sofas, and banquettes in a range of three complementary colors. Precast tables in matching black terrazzo sit on the dark walnut floor that runs though into the restaurant. The restaurant seats 70 people and features circular booths with backs of varying height, offering intimate tables. Angled mirrors mounted to the perimeter walls provide distorted glimpses of

fellow diners. While sufficiently removed from the lounge bar, the restaurant area can also be completely closed off by means of a full-height curtain.

The overall impact is of a strong, unique, and elegant environment through the thoughtful blend of modernity and a sense of timelessness The timeless design will enable Borough to age gracefully and retain its popularity for many years to come.

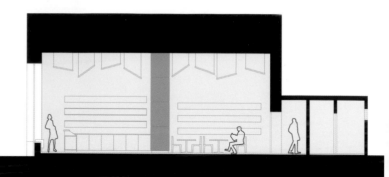

Section

bar counter

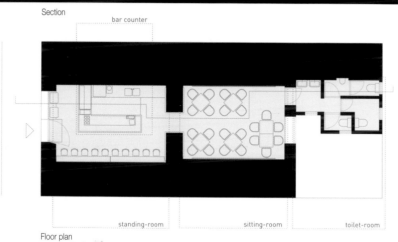

standing-room   sitting-room   toilet-room

Floor plan

Buffet Vinica

3LHD ARCHITECTS

This small bar that unexpectedly became a favorite hangout for Zagreb's local policemen was conceived from a very simple brief: the client wanted a central venue on a small budget.

Narrow, with high ceilings, and located in a downtown street, every patron can capture some flash of detail from outside. On both walls, three horizontal strips of mirrors capture and reflect this movement from the busy street. The eye follows activity wherever the patron stands. The main bar is standing room only, with a room at the back that offers seating. Dark and intimate, the images from the front are repeated on three of the same horizontal glass strips, but with photographs inside that capture movements of the street's activity. These are the mechanical reproductions of a lost ambience.

The ceilings are more than 4 meters high, which enabled the architects to hang an aluminum lamp installation. The pole-like lamps illuminate at two ends and are named 'zolja,' because their look and function is like that of the military shoulder rocket launcher of the same name. In contrast, two existing vertical column-like walls were clad in soft leather so that people may comfortably lean on them or touch them when passing by.

Club Bali

M 41 LH 2

The cruise ships M/S Serenade and the M/S Symphony, which journey between Helsinki and Stockholm each feature a 'Club Bali.'

The concept for the interior design of these clubs was to create a colorful and playful landscape, mixing elements from various 'dream locations': lush colors of tropical fauna and flora, the booming sound systems of beach parties under a starlit sky, aerial views of rich archipelagos, and islands in exotic locations.

People move through an archipelago where islands, each uniquely designed, serve as places for relaxing and chatting. The islands provide a variety of places, for both large parties and small groups that desire more intimate conversations.

During the day, this abstract landscape mixes visually with the actual archipelago of the Baltic Sea, seen through the windows. In the evening the focal point of the space turns inward, toward the dance floor. The DJ, operating from a structure resembling a volcano, sets the mood through music, lights, and video projections.

Photography: Janne Suhonen and Matti Pyykkö

Club F4

A cross-section of F4 reveals a rectangle with an angle void subtracted from it, a symmetrical diamond shape with a convex folded ceiling. Angled walls, ceiling, and tiered floor converge to a focal point, creating a false perspective. Elements reflect not only form but also function. For example, a chair need not only be a type of seating arrangement, but also a sculpture that stands alone as an art piece, linking it to the Bauhaus and Russian Constructivist ideals, the primary design influence. F4 creates the form, structure, and movement to allow patrons to become part of and interact with the venue. Organic materials, for example, stimulate a sense of well being, through sight, smell, and touch.

The main space within this venue revolves around the principle of functionality. The daily or weekly usage of F4 can be adapted to suit the needs of the clientele. Tiered flooring and ceiling give a theatrical feel to the whole place, creating depth and perspective as well as being useful when a seated function requires patrons to face one direction of the room. The bar is huge and central in its position, allowing for greater fluidity in access and service.

Overlooking the historic buildings of Little Collins Street, the members' room has its own semi-outdoor patio. Totally encased in glass, the members' area represents refinement and flair. Diacritic down-lights located at each end of the space wash boldly decorated walls, where axonometric illusions hand painted onto canvas evoke 1920's communist Russian poster art. This area can be dedicated for any private function or as a backstage area for a catwalk or live music situation.

Club Sugar

JOHN FRIEDMAN ALICE KIMM ARCHITECTS

Club Sugar was designed to both facilitate and confuse the voyeuristic and narcissistic activities of seeing, looking, and gazing, in an attempt to create a series of spaces that would not only enhance the conditions for desire in a sexually charged atmosphere, but whose very design would arouse the sensibilities of the club's patrons.

The design was initiated with the selection of numerous new plastic materials with the intention of exploiting their contradictory qualities of transparency and reflectivity, as well as varying degrees of translucency, distortion, and color. These hard materials were juxtaposed against softer and warmer materials such as drapery, exposed brick, and the exposed wood ceiling structure.

The dance floor is separated from the bar by a stainless steel coil screen that is closed at the beginning of each evening, so one sees an empty, but steam- and light-filled dance floor through it. As density increases in the bar, it is parted gradually until the club is full and it settles into its completely open position.

Floor plan

SIDEWALK

BROADWAY

Rest rooms are accessed by a polycarbonate-clad 'tunnel' that creates a distorted view of the dancers. Each of the restrooms has a clear acrylic door allowing direct views into the lavatory areas. The walls and ceilings of these spaces are of identically colored acrylic panels so that the patrons are enveloped in a warm, colored glow that the architects refer to as 'saturated psychological territories.' This is also true in the restrooms, where walls and ceilings are completely clad with identically colored mirrors. A slot in the wall between the men's and women's sides allows the lavatory counter to slip from one side to the next, as well as creating space for a peeping Tom or Jane to get a glimpse into the other side.

Crush Champagne Lounge

Crush Champagne Lounge was designed as a sophisticated lounge/bar aimed at attracting a discerning clientele. The objective was to create loungeroom 'pods' throughout the area where up to eight people could sit comfortably and converse in their own space. Large lights were installed over each grouping to further enhance the individual loungeroom concept. The soft gray and brown hues of the Milliken 'Oxygen' carpet, and sofas and settees designed by Bombast, Vancouver, are accented with splashes of color from the oversized orange day beds. Bubble lamps by Foscarini hang over the white Corian bar that runs the length of the room.

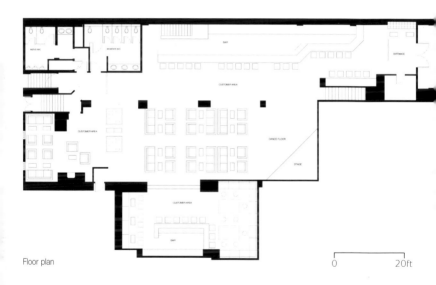

Floor plan

0   20ft

Dada

Dada is located on the ground level of a high-rise residential tower and has the most sought-after tables in Istanbul. On the ground floor, the bar and lounge section is furnished with a mirrored screen, a 5 meter long bench, and darbukas (a Turkish percussion instrument) as coffee tables. The area is illuminated by large chandeliers and tiny spots placed in between mirrored panels on the ceiling, made complete with the addition of large, comfortable leather armchairs to create a laid-back feeling.

The restaurant, located on the first floor, consists of three interconnecting sections; the main dining room, the VIP room, and the cozy room. White gauze curtains hang from a 6-meter-high ceiling, a large bookcase covers a wall, tables are illuminated by large pendant lights, and there are large sofas with cushions. The entire floor is decorated to reflect the glamour of yesteryear's mansions.

Ground floor plan

Distrikt Nightclub

SUPERKÜL INC. ARCHITECT WITH UW DESIGN GROUP INC.

The venue is located in Toronto's entertainment district among the theaters, restaurants, and multitude of nightclubs. It has a design that speaks of warmth, grandness, and cool. The entry sequence begins via an exterior stair that leads down to a long tunnel. The mood in the tunnel is subdued, lit by slivers of colored light emanating from slanted walls, at the end of which is a stair that leads up to the nightclub.

There are two VIP areas upstairs: the first has private, intimate banquettes, glass guards, and suspended glowing drink rails. The second, at the other end of the space, is raised and helps to contain the large dance floor. A 28-meter-long walnut bar connects the VIP areas. A sculpted ceiling hovering above reinforces the bar's presence in the space. Multi-colored beams of light shoot down from the ceiling onto the bar surface.

DR Bar

WOOD-ZAPATA, INC.

A quiet place for casual conversation and relaxation, the DR Bar offers fine wines, champagne, the best martini in Shanghai, and a collection of premium spirits. The interior design features works by many of the architects and designers who came together to create the distinctive contemporary Chinese style that has become synonymous with Xintiandi.

The DR in the name stands for 'design resources.' This small bar endeavors to promote awareness of some of the extraordinary design resources available in China. The designers (and owners) include the chief architect of Xintiandi, Ben Wood, and Francis Yum, the builder/producer of many of Xintiandi's best restaurants. All the materials, furniture, and finishes in the bar are from sources within mainland China. The millwork is matte-finish black lacquer, and the bar top and vodka trough is made from Tibetan silver mesh. The back bar is made using five slabs of Anhui ink stone, the ceiling is of Yunnan saddle leather, and the long wall is made from sliced Hang Zhou black roof tiles.

ED

DAVID LING ARCHITECT

Situated on the border between Soho and Greenwich Village, ED is a Hong Kong-style dim sum shop/sushi bar. Formerly a flaggling sushi bar suffering from post 9/11 doldrums, the owners asked for the restaurant to be totally re-branded with a new look for the existing 900-square-foot interior design, uniforms, menu, signage, and even music.

Originally an irregular space with nooks and crannies, a rectilinear space was formed, lined with sheets of pink backlit rear-projection screens. A waterfall with the appearance of flowing mercury is the axial focus of the symmetrical plan. Just in front is the altar-like sushi bar, sheathed in mirrored panels, flanked by gloss black latex banquettes, gloss black tables and clear acrylic chairs. The floors are mirrored acrylic, distressed to resemble silver leaf.

The uniforms are classic Chinese chi pao dresses, made kinky in shiny black latex. The signage is glowing neon behind sandblasted acrylic. Ghosted Chinese characters read congee, noodle, and rice. Menu items are listed in white Verdana on a gloss black background. Gunmetal glazed dishes complete the picture.

The bar is a stage for Ed, the sushi chef. As customers develop a personal relationship with Ed, the bar has become his stage, his podium and performance space. The bar contains slabs of fish and is clad in mirrors. Ed's 'audience' sits facing him on transparent acrylic chairs.

Including interiors, fashion, graphics and tabletop, the ED gesamtkunstwerk took five days to design and seven weeks to build.

Energie Bar

The Energie Bar is part of the Energie retail design store but has its own separate entrance. The bar serves as a brief pause during the day and a fashionable hangout at night. Small plasma screens offer a personal peek into the latest fashion and music trends.

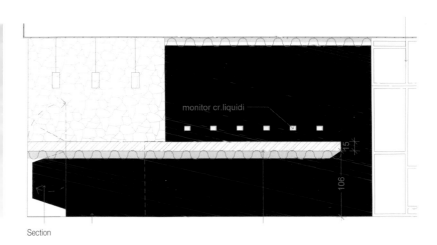

monitor cr.liquidi

15

106

Section

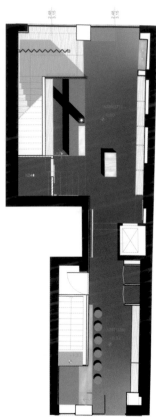

Bar and store plan

Energie Café

Completed in May 2003, the Energie Café in Catania is a lounge/bar and part of the Energie/Miss Sixty retail design store. It is located inside the store but has its own entrance as well. Traditional materials together with vintage pieces from the 1950s create this intimate and friendly atmosphere.

Located in one of the most vivid cities of Sicily, this is an interpretation of the old-fashioned bars and cafés that still exist in this area. They are called 'il circolo' in Italian, meaning the conversation circle: a place where people gather to talk about politics or soccer.

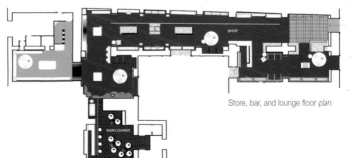

Store, bar, and lounge floor plan

Eve

The innovative team of artists and designers at Flux Design developed the interior theme of Eve. An elegant balance of taste and temptation accents this contemporary interpretation of the Garden of Eden. The graceful lines and contrasting textures of the design grew from a series of tables developed and built by Flux Design owners Jeremy Sham and Jesse Meyer. Their comparatively humble Hobbit Series tables sprung forth into sweeping entranceway and wall structures and trickled all the way down to the candleholders and door handles.

Completed in December 2001, nearly every interior feature of this upscale restaurant and nightclub was designed and handcrafted by Flux Design and took nearly one year to complete. The first-level restaurant and lounge is rich with organic lines and forms of hand-bent steel, featuring a backlit drinks bar with a layered concrete and glass top, supported by more than 50 miniature steel trees. More than 170 concrete forms were poured and beautifully finished for the bar tops, drink rails, dining tables, and bathroom sinks.

The upper-level nightclub is notably contemporary, with geometric yet whimsical structures. The two bars, along with the DJ booth and dance platform, are noted by crisp contrasts of shape, texture, and color. A twisting steel sculpture snakes out of the floor from the garden below and leads from room to room as it swallows aluminum orbs along its path.

Photography: courtesy
Flux Design

117

eve

DAVID HICKS PTY LTD

This nightclub and bar was inspired by a desire to create something that was a new look for a venue in Australia. Influence was drawn from the disco eras of the 1970s and early 1980s when going out was a glamorous event. As the space was located in a basement, external influences were not necessary to be considered. The aim was to create a world of escape. Once inside the space, patrons could be anywhere: in a disco, on a 1970's cruise ship, in New York at Studio 54 or in a glamorous hotel in Las Vegas. The fantasy of transporting people into different periods, cities, and environments was a big inspiration.

For effect, Kreon Inlites and chandeliers were used for lighting. The tables were custom-designed and bongo drums were added. The wallpaper was selected from the range of Florence Broadhurst signature prints. To create warmth, timber and carpet were used in the flooring.

Photography: Trevor Mein

Fusion Bar and Lounge

The client requested a design that was unpretentious, comfortable, warm, and sensual with a retro-Cuban feel. Working with the limited construction budget of US$32,000, the architects used simple materials, bold colors, and dynamic lighting to create a rich atmosphere.

To emphasize the long and narrow space, River Architects designed a bar that angled out of the southern wall and gradually led patrons into the cozy lounge in the back. To accommodate the narrow bar area and to relate to the mid-century modern furniture, the padded-vinyl bar front was designed to cushion the knees against the hard surface of the wood. One aged cast-iron column caked with paint, located by the front windows, was left untouched. Since the new ceiling level had to drop below its capital, the ceiling was framed around the capital, accenting it with a hidden light. A cozy Cuban cigar lounge was emulated for that retro-Cuban feel.

Photography: Juhee Lee-Hartford and James Hartford

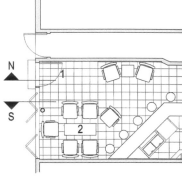

Floor plan

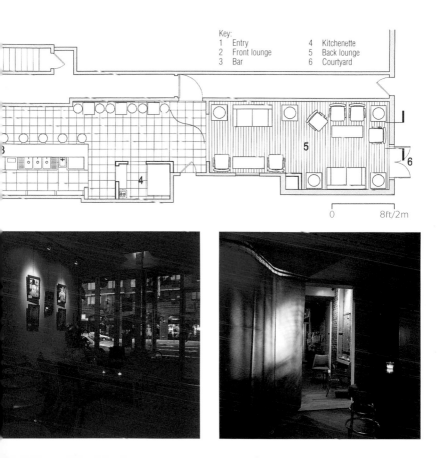

Key:
1 Entry
2 Front lounge
3 Bar
4 Kitchenette
5 Back lounge
6 Courtyard

0   8ft/2m

GLO Bar

BATES SMART PTY LTD

GLO was designed to be the signature cocktail lounge and visual centerpiece of the main gaming floor at Sydney's Star City Casino. Set in a sea of hyperactivity and high energy, its unique design allows it to transcend its surrounds to achieve a sense of relaxed sophistication.

GLO is set on a viewing platform surrounded by a patterned metal screen, enhancing the sense of elegance and luxury delivered by high-end finishes and opulent fabrics. GLO invokes a sense of theater through the spectacular diaphanous 100-meter-long chandelier that spirals down over the lounge area, creating a dramatic and seductive atmosphere. The chandelier is composed of 2-meter-long acrylic rods suspended from a 6.8-meter-high ceiling lit by fiber optics.

This exquisite bar realizes a level of sophistication unsurpassed in both context and form. Patrons can circulate and communicate in a seductive environment unparalleled in any other urban setting.

With its ambience, lit by the truly breathtaking chandelier, GLO achieves what so many strive for: delivering a real experience to patrons. Its design and location make it a haven for casino guests looking for respite and sophistication, and what better respite from the hustle and bustle of the gaming floor than a five-star 1950's style cocktail lounge.

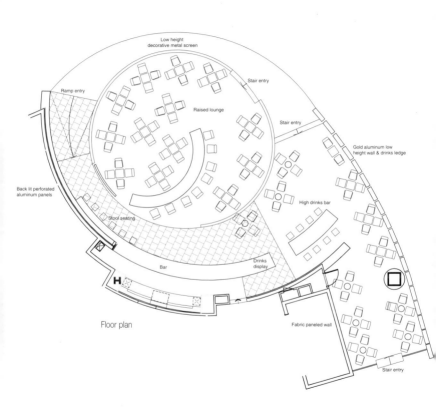

Low height
decorative metal screen

Stair entry

Ramp entry

Stair entry

Raised lounge

Gold aluminum low
height wall & drinks ledge

Back lit perforated
aluminum panels

High drinks bar

Stool seating

Bar

Drinks
display

Floor plan

Fabric paneled wall

Stair entry

Guillaume at Bennelong

DALE JONES-EVANS PTY LTD ARCHITECTURE

The re-design of Guillaume at Bennelong involved the use of light to reinforce the drama and scale of the ribbed shell structure of the Opera House that encases the restaurant. While reinforcing this overwhelming architectural gesture, it was necessary to design a low layer of intimacy, which was achieved using light. A series of small- and large-scale lamps were designed and placed throughout to ensure that an intimate and sensually illuminated ambience occurred.

The architect collaborated with Australian indigenous artists to introduce a direct and abstract sense of aboriginality throughout the space. The aboriginal elements: large- and small-scale painted lamps (painted by Central Desert, Utopia, artist Barbara Weir) and the hollow log-painted memorial poles (*larrakitj*) from the Yolnu people of Gove Peninsula, appear to come from the land below the Opera House and penetrate the ground plane of Utzon's architecture. The eight *larrakitj* (also approached as objet d'art) command center space under the shell, like Captain Cook's flag which was stuck into the shores of Botany Bay more than 200 years ago. The lamps and *larrakitj* seek to remind us of the aboriginal place on which the Opera House and restaurant now stand.

Photography: Paul Gosney

Three terraces flow in open plan from the upper-level cocktail bar. The mid-level central bar is flanked by two large sculpted bronzed vases designed to carry Australian flower arrangements (by Sydney's floral artiste, Grandiflora). The *larrakitj* are also located at the center and heart of the ribbed-shell structure. The color palette of fabrics, furniture, and joinery ranges from muddy browns to saffron orange and anchors the space in contrast to Utzon's white shells. The color scheme also reduces glare and over lighting and generates a layer of warmth for the restaurant.

Floor plan

Helsinki Club

M41LH2

M41LH2 created a luscious and rich atmosphere in one of Helsinki's oldest nightspots, with the assistance of designers from the agency Anteeksi. Together, they refurbished the interior (with the exception of the restrooms and the entrance) of what was originally a 1970's nightclub and casino.

With the use of opulent carpet, mirrors, and gold wallpaper, the new interior appears luxurious and inviting, giving life and warmth to the space. The main dance floor is located beneath a glazed ceiling and features a white bar—a stark contrast to the red and orange tones of the other areas. A lounge room and VIP room continue this color scheme, while the 'back room' features vintage furniture, decorated entirely by the staff for their own use.

Photography: Matti Pyykkö

149

Key:
1 Entrance
2 Bar island (the dome)
3 Central lounge
4 Casino
5 The tunnel (the tram)
6 Main dance area

Floor plan

0   32ft/10m

Herzblut

JORDAN MOZER AND ASSOCIATES, LIMITED WITH UDO ULRICH

Herzblut was developed to promote Astra Beer for Strenger's clients at the Holsten Brewery in Hamburg. The Astra Beer logo is a heart with an anchor inscribed in it, a celebration of the harbor neighborhood where the beer is brewed. This area is noted for the Reeperban: the famous street filled with theaters and cabarets, and the place where the Beatles played their earliest shows.

The façade and interior are warm, a modern take on an old tavern with surprising details. Inspired by the curve of the hulls of big ships in the Hamburg harbor, the façade is composed of steel reinforcing and painted concrete with front doors made of rusty steel.

Two arches near the entry are made of glass Bisazza tiles. The stripes suggest the jerseys worn by the St. Pauli football club, one of the sponsors of Herzblut. The illuminated mural, composed and manufactured by Jordan Mozer and Associates, Limited (JMA) along the wall is a series of hearts, another riff on the Astra logo.

The façade and many of the interior walls, are composed of traditional plaster. The plaster forms were designed on computer, then sent via email to Martin Ranft, a master-plasterer, who developed the framing elements at his studio near Frankfurt and shipped them to Hamburg where they were set in place, tied together with lathe, and plastered by hand.

Photography: Klaus Frahm

The floor, the bar, and the seating are composed of smoked oak. The light fixtures, composed of spun metal, cast resin, etched acrylic, and blown glass, were designed and fabricated in Chicago and shipped to Hamburg. The back bar shelving is also composed of cast aluminum-magnesium alloy brackets with wood shelves created especially for Herzblut by JMA. The railings are made of raw steel, suggestive of the materials in the Hamburg shipyards. Custom barstools were made by JMA in raw steel tube for the project.

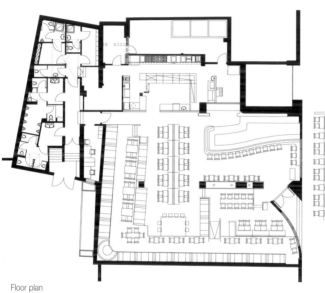

Floor plan

Himmelreich

JMA was responsible for the development of the design for the new Karstadt Lifestyle Prototype Department store. Himmelreich is located within the women's fashion zone. The venue features a very long bar, which has a parallel bar-height banquette, encouraging density. The café area is filled with tables and overlooks the street, while the lounge area is toward the rear. The café is accessible from the parking lot, so it can remain open later than the store, operating as a separate business.

The ceiling of Himmelreich was built in plaster, and is composed of four different melted and perforated planes. Like most of Jordan Mozer's projects, there are a number of elements that were designed exclusively for the project. The light fixtures and enormous curved and perforated lanterns were designed in CAD in Chicago and cut using CAM in Germany, and then sanded and lacquered. The flooring, composed of Amtico vinyl tile, was also designed this way.

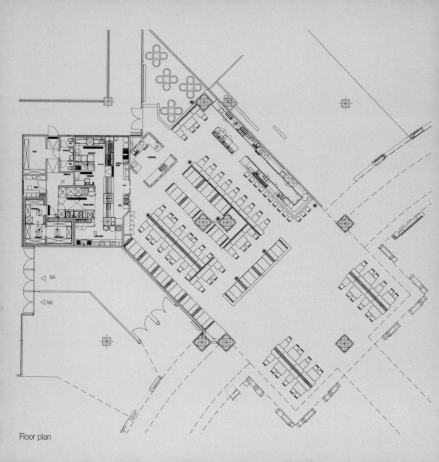

Floor plan

HUDSON
CLUB
RESTAURANT & BAR

MON-FRI OPEN AT 3:00
SAT. OPEN AT 5:00
SUN - CLOSED

Hudson Club

JORDAN MOZER AND ASSOCIATES, LIMITED

The owners asked JMA to assist them in the development of a modern American brasserie and bar that would offer 'flights' of wine. The new environment was to be a mixture of 'tomorrow' and 'once upon a time', with an emphasis on the 1930s. During its research the design team became transfixed not by the architecture of the period, but by the design of airplanes, dirigibles, and fantasies about spacecraft.

The existing building was built like an airplane hangar, with 75-foot-long wooden trusses in the ceiling. One long speedy room was developed with terraces and rooms opening onto it. Wings sprouted from walls and window openings became 'pushed' ovals, egg-like—inspired by blurred photographs of airplane windows in flight, and by the dynamic forms of teardrops, airplane wing sections, and whales. A sense of movement and flight was invoked for the design of chairs and barstools, again employing sections used in airplane fuselage and tail design.

Photography: Doug Snower and David Clifton

165

Lucky Strike

SFJONES ARCHITECTS

Material was salvaged from the interior of a long-running bowling alley before it was torn down and reused for this project. Lane 16 from the old venue formed the new bar top and some of the furniture was designed using various other parts of leftover lanes. The Hollywood sign and the stars, once used as movie props, were also rescued.

The new Hollywood venue is located in a basement space that has its own street entrance. A 9-meter bowling pin hangs from the side of the wall outside the door. Inside, photographed art is projected on large screens at the end of the lanes. These images are synchronized with a DJ stand that plays music and coordinates the art images on the screens.

Floor plan, Orange County

Malmaison Birmingham

JESTICO + WHILES

Malmaison is a boutique hotel brand. Its unique character is defined by a blend of Scottish origins and strong continental influences, namely the 19th-century French château Malmaison, whose name and image it borrows.

Malmaison is a highly individual and stylish hotel group so it was important that the architects responded to the established core values, but also take them forward to a new chapter. .

The Mailbox building's steel structure has allowed for more generous spaces, particularly in the front of house areas. Jestico + Whiles embraced this opportunity to open the space and created a magnificent double-height bar with a large raspberry-red backlit glass backdrop and soaring double-height bar and brasserie that become the heart of the hotel. In contrast, the soft niches have a real fire at one end, and high-back signature chairs by the window at the opposite end. The window in the bar area is dressed with full-height wooden blinds that feel both welcoming and impressive. The bar offers a modern, yet relaxing, urban drinking spot.

Mars Lounge

DAVID HICKS PTY LTD

Located at the end of Oxford Street and the edge of Surry Hills, the existing building had many intriguing features. Timber ceiling beams, existing timber flooring, and feature brickwork walls were maintained and incorporated into the scheme. This gave the area a lofty warehouse feel that provides a project contrast with streamlined insertions of silver and black glitter bar boxes, a drinking bench, and circular Vivid White gloss and red-lined seating pods. The red links the space back to the Mars theme and makes it exciting, vibrant, and contemporary.

The venue's warehouse feel was further emphasized with a glamorous undertone highlighted with slick detailing. Contrasting materials were used to bring warmth to the space while still maintaining a high level of design resolution. Materials and paint colors were chosen to highlight the venue's modernism—metal mixed with timber mixed with stone, and shiny mixed with matt mixed with rough. This was achieved with the Burmese Beige wall render and slick insertions of Vivid White, Deep Onyx, and punches of Cherry Red.

This blend provides a stimulating environment to be in, both on a visual and tactile level. The various seating arrangements allow patrons to stand and have a beer, lounge and sip a cocktail, or sit and dine. For those who get itchy feet, dancing is encouraged on top of the drinking bench.

Photography: Kyle Ford

179

Mingara

The brief for Mingara was to create a timeless and individual interior, with a tropical yet sophisticated feel that would appeal to a patron demographic ranging from 18 through to 80 years old

The design concept combines the color palette of the local NSW central coast and the simple and elegant design detailing found in a tropical resort or hotel. A palette of natural coastal blues, greens and aqua colors complements more earthy browns and burnt oranges. Color has been used sparingly to create the most impact and to contrast against a refreshing clean white backdrop.

The club consists of a series of large barrel-vaulted spaces that have an inherent commercial aesthetic. Ambient lighting, soft furnishings, and warm tactile finishes have been used to visually soften the existing structure. To create a more intimate feel, suspended ceiling elements hang within the barrel vaults, bringing ceilings down to a human scale as well as accentuating the unusual height and volume of the spaces. To add a sense of theater and entertainment to the patron's journey through the club, PDT superimposed a more organic pathway that meanders through the building.

Photography: Christine Wood and Karl Hofman

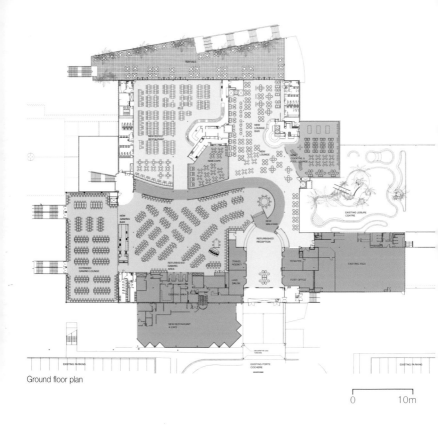

Ground floor plan

Part-height partitions were used throughout the fitout, allowing patrons to make a visual connection between spaces, while still allowing each area to have an individual look. Because of the huge variety of different people that visit the club, it was important that there was a certain level of visual transparency between areas.

Simplistic design was exploited to accentuate and focus attention on carefully planned feature elements within the design. This has given the space a sense of integrity and refreshing visual clarity that gives the club its own unique experience.

Nasa

JOHANNES TORPE STUDIOS

The owners of two of Copenhagen's most successful clubs desired a true 'members only' venue with a small but well-chosen audience, and a quality and level of service that would please the royals, the models, and the popstars: a pearl of design never seen before.

Science-fiction films of the 1960s inspired the outstanding original design. Although the interior is reminiscent of the past, Nasa established a new standard in nightclub design in the late 1990s. Everything from the ashtrays to the toilet doors is customized for Nasa.

Nasa is the only completely white nightclub in the world, or as the English lifestyle magazine *Wallpaper* says, 'Nasa is a hermetic obsessively white club with a glass lift to beam up in—it makes London's Pharmacy (a bar/club) look like Boots—the chemist.'

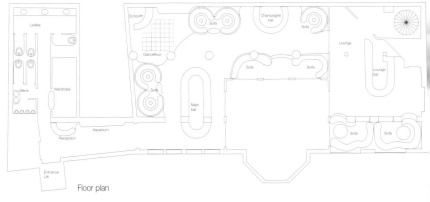

Floor plan

Nectar

JORDAN MOZER AND ASSOCIATES, LIMITED

When asked to develop a bar in the Nevada desert, the design team came up with an image of melting forms. They created a single food and beverage facility for simple, fresh seasonal food with two distinct parts to balance one another: a yin yang idea— a contrast between the two halves making a complete whole.

A German team that usually restores old European churches manually plastered CAD-CAM sculpted framing for the walls and ceiling. A hand-sculpted bar, of seamless terrazzo—fused with blue glass shards—melts down to create a floor. The barstools were also CAD-CAM sculpted and cast in Kevlar-reinforced non-combustible resin, and with cast aluminum–magnesium foot rests. The tabletops are composed of hand-polished glass mosaics set into cast-aluminum, magnesium-alloy frames, with a base of the same metal. The back bar cabinets are also CAD-CAM sculpted, with inset panels of poured art glass.

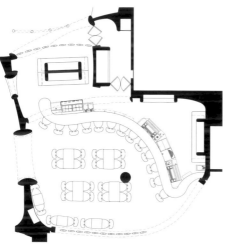

Partial floor plan

Nobu

GABELLINI ASSOCIATES

Nobu opened in conjunction with the 100,000-square-foot Armani Center in Milan. It involved an interesting collaboration between the two business partners, Giorgio Armani and Nobu Matsuhisa, and Gabellini Associates. The venue includes a large lounge and sake bar, a sushi bar, and a 130-seat dining area. Occupying a discreet corner of the Center primarily dedicated to service activities, Nobu's public façade is on the interior overlooking the Galleria Rotonda. Its corner location occupies both the ground and first levels, allowing its interior façade of taut clear glass panels and stacked stone piers to conceptually penetrate the floor.

The ground level features a large lounge area with a communal bar table, built-in bench seating with flexible cushions, and custom tables and chairs. The chairs and cushions were designed in collaboration with Vladimir Kagan. Natural materials and various subtle lighting techniques bathe the area in warm ambient light. A floor of closely spaced pietra serena stone slats folding onto stone piers, American walnut wall panels and furniture, natural plaster walls and ceilings, and bronze details provide a rich palette of materials.

Photography: courtesy Gabellini Associates and Bruna Ginammi

The main restaurant, located on the first level, is accessible through a double-height atrium lined in walnut panels enclosing a floating walnut stair. The main focus of the restaurant is the sushi bar, constructed of walnut, bronze, clear glass, and translucent onyx panels that emit a welcoming glow. Sliding translucent panels offer the option to subdivide the space for private dining.

Onesixone

Onesixone is an established Melbourne nightclub that has recently been transformed and extended to cater for a growing but discerning clientele. Located in the thick of Chapel Street's hectic commercial zone, the operators set out to create a sensual plush venue, offering exceptional service with a friendly and intimate ambience.

A narrow stair lit by an original 1960's glass chandelier greets patrons as they enter the venue. Flocked wallpaper adorns the club's walls and fluted timber paneling lines the bar front and the many seating alcoves. Toward the dance area, light, movement, and volume build up to the appearance of one of Australia's first flashing dance floors since the death of disco. Recycled basketball-court flooring has been used to line the walls, padded panels, and seating. Fish tanks are located above lounge areas, in washrooms, and over corridors, and specialist neon lighting is used throughout.

The new lower-level bar reflects the same tongue-in-cheek design elements, with the use of black acid-etched mirrors, and retro light fittings and wallpaper.

Oscar's Bar at Andel's Hotel

JESTICO + WHILES

Following the success of its internationally acclaimed One Aldwych and The Hempel in London, Vienna International appointed Jestico + Whiles as interior designer of its new-build hotel at Andel City.

The 280-bedroom hotel is designed to be the social heart of Andel City, and will bring hotel 'lobby culture' to Prague for the first time.

The ground floor café bar at Andel's has become Prague's most fashionable new venue. Both guests and city dwellers alike gather to experience the cool atmospheric space in the established tradition of the hotel lobby.

Studded with glowing white glass cubes and with slots lined with blood-red glass, a wall of random coursed slate stands in contrast to the polished stone bar counter. Against this eye-catching and theatrical backdrop, the most talented of barmen serve extravagant cocktails and the best coffee in town.

An elliptical shell, partially enclosed with shimmering metallic voile offers an intimate and sheltered atmosphere. For those who want to be seen, high glass tables are placed in the windows, beneath a huge, glowing spiral copper light.

Photography: Ales Jungmann

Panacea Nightclub

MCINTOSH PORIS ASSOCIATES

This corner building at West Congress and Shelby was in a dilapidated state prior to renovation. Originally a bank when completed in 1924, there were repeated, ill-advised renovations and many tenants from the 1970s onward, including fast food restaurants, delis, and cafés.

The architect's solution embraced the existing original elements, including an outstanding Moorish Revival terra cotta and limestone exterior with a second-floor perimeter arcade, a curved sliding bronze entry door, concrete structural columns, and a mezzanine-level bank manager's office. What was not readily apparent was uncovered through careful archeology. The most prized find was the building's original suspended plaster ceiling with its hand-stenciled detailing that covers two-thirds of the space.

The architects retained and restored these elements, accentuating the contrast between the historic and the contemporary. The sand-blasted exterior is representative of its original, exotic, and elaborate façade, which now looks refreshed during the day. During club hours, the windows are lit, throwing the façade into silhouette. Clubbers enter to find an intimate space consisting of a dance floor, bars, lounge areas, entry stair, and service areas.

Patrons interact with the selected finishes of wood, metal, and concrete, and with various elements, such as leather benches, plastic sofas, cloth pod seating, and high bar chairs. In a more ephemeral way, they dance in the spotlight or converse in the shadows. Through careful restoration and sensitive addition of material, provocative new life is brought to the site. Archeology meets techno.

Rain

II BY IV DESIGN ASSOCIATES INC.

The clients wanted a sophisticated destination that was ultra-cool and sensually inviting: a glamorous upscale cocktail lounge where the city's chic set would come to be seen.

The lounge area is furnished with small, armless couches, surrounding a central feather pouf covered in transparent vinyl. A top-lit suspended ceiling of stretched plastic adds human scale and reinforces the formal geometric planning below. This room is warmed by the glow of a circular cluster of fat white bulbs suspended through the canopy's central cut-out.

Clear bands in frosted glass partitions reveal the small dining room, which features a long, bar-height communal table, also constructed of stainless steel and frosted glass, and internally lit. Its rear wall comprises divider screens of 3-inch diameter bamboo canes embedded in concrete bases, bringing a touch of natural texture into the sleek surroundings.

Black vinyl seating units and white tables are set against the stunning, theatrically lit brick wall. Frosted glass dividers separate the dining rooms from the large lounge area, which features two bold internally lit white glass structures, a 20-seat service bar, and matching 8-seat drinks bar. A water feature, that seems to trickle among the display bottles, backs the glass panel and glass shelves of the back bar.

Photography: David Whittaker

With deflected and reflected light as the key design elements, this dramatic interior is simultaneously evocative of a misty lakeside, all softly gleaming shapes and mysterious shadows, and of an utterly urban and sophisticated setting—the perfect backdrop for sparkling conversation.

Saratoga

GRANT AMON ARCHITECTS PTY LTD

The Saratoga nightclub fitout is a complete reworking of an existing underground bar in Melbourne's South Yarra district. The treatment is lush, employing deep purples and reds with gold highlights throughout the expanded space. The existing main bar has been reclad with a backlit purple Marblo top and vinyl padded front. Behind the bar, the drink display features gold-trimmed shelving units mounted on a black mirror backing.

A smaller bar is located in an opposite corner, expanding service and capacity and providing intimacy. The gold laminate bar sits on red carpet and is surrounded by handmade dimpled tiles and bronzed mirror wall cladding. New chocolate banquette seating has been installed throughout the club in the lounge and booth areas.

The glitz continues, somewhat deliberate and cheesy, with platinum mosaic tiles and gold doors to the unisex bathrooms, the large sunset poster wall, ornate gold mirrors, and other lush tactics all set to swirl deliciously around the central DJ booth. While undeniably tilting its felt hat to the 1970s, Saratoga has been reborn for the new millennium to entertain the masses.

Photography: Trevor Mein and Richard Briglia

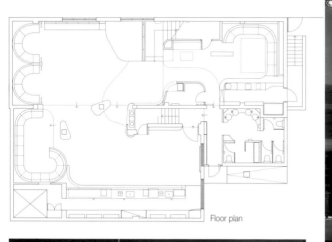

Floor plan

Seven

A concrete shell, over two levels buried within a distinctive five-level 1970's office building in South Melbourne became the raw beginnings for Seven. This shell was to house a major contemporary entertainment venue, consisting of ground floor entry, bar, dance zone, stage and service areas with a smaller upper level lounge, intimate bar/dance area and some funky restrooms. A robust steel and concrete stair partially encased in perforated mesh and red glass connects both levels.

The strategy developed along the concept of spatial manipulation of formal objects, where the objects themselves are transformed through material, texture, and light. The liquid flow of surfaces and form yields at times to abstraction and distortion, becoming subtle animated events adding depth and illusion to the other world of club dwellers. Materials such as translucent fiberglass, pearlized resin, and holographic and metallic vinyl rim the space for the main event of DJ, light show, and music

Photography: Richard Briglia & Shania Shegedyn

227

Upstairs, respite is available in the gold and purple padded-fabric enclosure of the lounge, given a soft glowing depth with a ceiling of stretched Japanese paper panels and dark mirror reflections. The triangular panels are backlit and perform a subtle fold, issuing an origami-like treatment of the surface. The red glass walls of the stairwell produce a backdrop to the bar of deep pink resin and tortoise-shell fiberglass. Beyond, rich timber paneled walls are literally compressed and folded into the main space, punctuated by light slits and pink resin ledges. The room that houses the omnipresent DJ booth is rimmed in a jade metallic-vinyl banquette and framed by gold reflective panels. Behind the panels, a unisex restroom of anonymous cubicles completes the facilities.

First floor plan

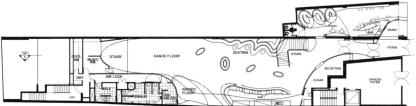

Ground floor plan

Seven

II BY IV DESIGN ASSOCIATES INC.

Asked to create the perfect setting for a high-energy nightclub in a flexible venue, that also generates revenue through corporate and private rentals, II BY IV chose to let the sound and light show—and the guests themselves—animate the space, rather than elaborate design details.

Located in the heart of the entertainment district, the site was an office building already occupied by the owner. To accommodate the new club, a fourth floor was added, connected to the third level by an internal staircase. The seven deadly sins provide the core interior theme through spectacular lighting effects (lust: blue, pride: violet, envy: green, gluttony: orange, anger: red, greed: yellow, sloth: light blue). These references are repeated throughout the facility.

A 30-foot internally lit bar is backed by a shallow counter in white epoxy lacquer, topped by an integrated stainless drink rail and bottle display surface that curves up to the ceiling to frame the mirrored wall above. Once again, the names of the sins are sandblasted into the mirror surface and backlit in continuously changing color, matched by downlighting on the bottle display.

Whether bathed in periwinkle, fuchsia or sunset-orange light, this remarkably minimalist white interior pulsates with personality, in an intimately scaled, manageable multipurpose venue that invites guests to explore its possibilities.

Photography: David Whittaker

231

Slate Bar and Billiards

WEISZ + YOES ARCHITECTURE

Named after the slate beneath the green felt on a pool table, the materials and architecture forms are derived from the geometric forms that feature in the game. The two former pool halls have been transformed into unique venues that combine billiards with fine dining and cocktails. They are large spaces that were gut renovated in order to provide a new design for each location.

Slate Queens features a 50-foot, custom designed serpentine crackle-glass bar with fiber optics, and a pool-ball shaped fireplace. The bars were developed out of special layers of laminated cracked glass above a hollow light table that held skeins of fiber optic cable.

Slate Chelsea also has this signature bar. A structural glass staircase in the shape of a pool triangle connects its two floors.

Both venues feature DJ booths and provide ambience for lounging, eating, and playing pool. Metal fabric curtains and a tensile fabric ceiling separate the eating and playing areas. Commercial kitchens were added to enable these venues to have full menus and cater for special events.

Photography: Paul Warchol

235

Floor plan

Stars

A circular bench and small high-grade steel tables invite the visitor to relax in the lounge area. The walls and ceiling, bar, and shelves are painted white and appear to visually meld together. Silver metal wall-lights can be dimmed, turning the room's atmosphere from cool to warm as desired.

The hall shifts to smoky charcoal-colored walls, ceilings, and floor. The room's furnishing elements create a contrast and their unified white colors emphasize their transformation into sculptural bodies designed with round edges. On the dance floor, the colors change again through the use of orange lights.

The rear wall has a circular depression, 3.6 meters in diameter, with a surface that subtly curves to the inside. Different planets, with their surfaces changed through computer animation, spin around their own axes. The concave wall design emphasizes the perception of three-dimensional animated planets and seduces one into a world of imagination.

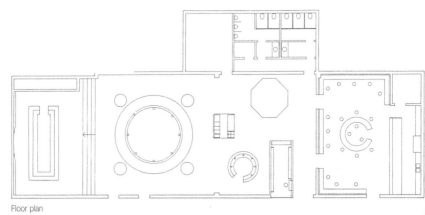

Floor plan

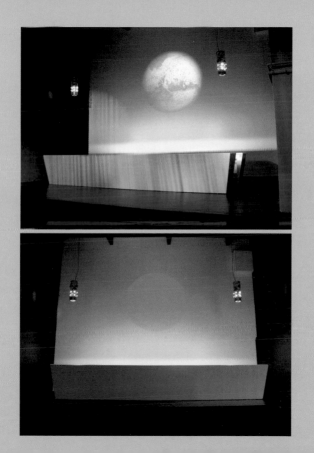

Sudhaus

Sudhaus is located in a popular summer holiday resort. Its first room features a sculptured bar that winds itself around the central staircase. Machined parts were pulled over specifically designed templates and the material was welded together on site. The vertical elements of the bar are made of walnut. Rays of light fall through the wooden blinds hanging from the high windows facing the street throughout the day and night.

The first-floor lounge is furnished with soft brown leather sofas, varnished side tables, and leather stools. The second-floor bar is painted dark brown, and contains a smaller cubic bar, made of highly polished high-grade steel, combined with walnut.

Photography: Rudolf Schnellbach

SuperGeil

JOHANNES TORPE STUDIOS

Designed to be developed as a future café chain with international locations, SuperGeil is currently one of Copenhagen's most unusual and eye-catching cafés. Design, lifestyle, and leisure industry magazines from all over the world have reviewed it. In addition to its good-looking interior, it is simply a pleasant place to eat, drink, and play.

The development of the SuperGeil chain was stalled by a troubled economy after the September 11 attacks in the United States. Investors are optimistic and plan to start the chain up again by opening new cafés throughout the European Union.

Photography: Jens Stolze

supperclub

Amsterdam's supperclub is divided into four different rooms: la Salle Neige, le Bar Rouge, le Salon Colore, and les Toilettes Noir.

The main restaurant is located in la Salle Neige, an all white two level space in which colored lights change the appearance of the room, and video projections decorate the walls. Visitors dine from silver metal trays while resting on huge white mattresses that run along the two main walls. In the center of the room there is the option of more conventional table dining on Verner Panton chairs at round tables. An open kitchen is located at the back where waiters serve the five-course set meal.

The retro-style le Bar Rouge holds up to 60 people and features red curtains and a big neon 'bar' sign. Les Toilettes Noir, the restrooms, feature giant rubber cubes in the center where people can sit and chat. Finally, le Salon Colore can be found in the basement and is designed for those who like to just lounge and relax.

supperclub cruise

CONCRETE ARCHITECTURAL ASSOCIATES

The creators of Amsterdam's supperclub have taken the original concept and transported it to the water: a floating nightclub that can either travel on the waterways to pick up its patrons, or stay docked.

The ship can be divided into three main areas: entrance and restrooms, La Salle Neige, and Le Bar Noir. Each has a different feel and color, as their names suggest.

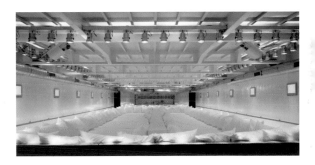

Photography: courtesy Concrete Architectural Associates

Tea Factory Bar and Kitchen

WELLS MACKERETH

The site occupies the ground floor of a steel-framed brick warehouse. The client required a bar large enough for 600 people with DJ area, seating, and restaurant space as well as associated back-of-house and service areas. The aim was to attract an urban crowd that would dress down to go out rather than 'smarten up'. This lent itself to the feel of the vacant site, with its concrete and brick finishes and grand-scaled exposed steel-riveted structure.

The architects organized the main bar along the center of one side wall, making the most of the linear nature of the interior, and using the existing brick finish as a backdrop to the activity of the bar and bottle display. Wells Mackereth exploited the use of materials in a raw form to suit the 'warehouse feel' of the project: galvanized ductwork, 'gunmetal' finish to the steel structure, natural render wall, and the asphalt floor finish. The latter has been highly polished to give a 'just-poured appearance, almost like an oil slick. The steel-framed modules of the light boxes have inset twin-wall polycarbonate sheeting, a material more commonly used in factory roofing.

Carefully inserted warm materials contrast with hard finishes, seen in the use of natural walnut for the bar cladding, stairs and restaurant seating area, the felt-clad panels, the large leather sofas, and the dark brown coir matting which runs the full width of the seating area.

Terrace Bar

FLUX DESIGN

Owners David Larson and Nick Howell were looking for a distinctive way to employ minimal materials in a location that demanded a careful and intelligent integration of form and function. The crisp contemporary building rises out of a row of Irish pubs on Milwaukee's Water Street strip.

The site is physically narrow (less than 20 feet across) but the space feels much larger than it actually is. Steel and concrete tables seem to slip right out of the walls and pulsate with the same lighting effect as the building's façade. The bars rise from the floor, beneath dramatic canopies of faux-finished plastic, while the liquor shelves pop out of the concrete block walls. The stairs and two sub-level balconies are lined with steel mesh cast in textured translucent plastic that transmits the changing lights and passing figures.

Three garage-style doors slide open and add to the openness of the space and a breathtaking view of the Milwaukee skyline can be taken in from the rooftop patio. Terrace is testimony that cramped locations so often overlooked or dismissed can be dramatic and comfortable venues.

Photography: Rockstar Design and Todd Dacquisto

The Brig

JOHN FRIEDMAN ALICE KIMM ARCHITECTS

Presented with a run-down, 52-year-old landmark bar with an exterior mural, the architect's aim was to intensify the building's ability to act as a gateway to Venice, maintain the original ad hoc quality of the bar's interior, and create a public space with a mood that welcomes the diverse spirit of the city. This project is a combination of the raw and refined, the old and new, the highly deliberate and ad hoc. It maintains the edginess of the original bar while adding a new sensuality and fluidity.

Photography: Benny Chan / Fotoworks

The simplicity of the interior plan belies the richness and diversity of materials: colors that simultaneously allow the bar to maintain its original character while appealing to its new patrons. Unifying all elements of the space is the pink and purple terrazzo that forms the ceiling, walls, and floors of the restrooms before it spills out in olive green to cover the floor areas outside. Similarly straddling the crude and the refined is a ceiling of plastic laminate panels suspended over the bar in a standard T-bar ceiling grid. Lit from above, it gives off a sensuous glow that provides much of the bar's mood.

Compressed between the floor and ceiling are a variety of wall surfaces. Of special note is the molded linoleum wallpaper that wraps the freestanding bathroom volumes at the end of the space. Dripping with silver paint, these volumes serve as silent witness to the events unfolding in front of them. Also effective is the 'miniskirt' of glowing sheer white fabric that hangs beneath the bar. Finally, a 14-foot-long steel table with a circular ashtray that moves in and out of one of the bar's two front doors is crucial to the identity of the project.

The Garden

STUDIOACHT.

The Garden is situated near Theresienwiese, home of the famous Oktoberfest. A brilliant green light on the exterior and a soft light shining through the entry doors are the only indication that there is a nightclub inside the otherwise plain building.

The main bar is constructed from natural stone and walnut, with a soft-form ceiling above. An indoor garden featuring Japanese bamboo trees, grass, and volcanic stones is located opposite the bar. A movable stage features red curtains that can be closed during live acts.

The lounge area is raised and furnished with comfortable seats and small handmade high-grade steel tables. The backstage area features a small bathroom, a wardrobe with tall mirrors, and a small private lounge for the musicians, which is furnished with divans.

SYDNEY, NEW SOUTH WALES, AUSTRALIA

theloft and bungalow 8

DALE JONES-EVANS PTY LTD ARCHITECTURE

Commissioned as one project, the brief required two spaces with two identities that would operate independently and be physically linked (the Link is a common stair that can be subdivided with a bamboo gate). One kitchen would service both spaces.

bungalow 8's ambience comes from a painterly materiality and interaction with light sources. The warm 'off black-brown' textured and lacquered space, washed with differential low levels of illuminated and reflective light act as a seductive painting. This golden colored light paints the reversed split-faced bamboo and stained-rattan walls.

The long bar runs parallel with the water's edge and buries itself deeply within the cool recesses of the building, a retreat from the light and heat. The open kitchen was planned to have immediate address with the public domain as well as the interior space. This project utilizes quite common materials and has acoustic treatment throughout.

theloft is a lunch and dinner tapas bar, and a cocktail bar by night. The space is precious and ornate, rich in color and texture, with oversized couches. Furniture is over-scaled, padded and cigar-like, soft, and comfortable. Dani Marti, a rope artist, collaborated with the architects to produce a large wall piece.

Photography: Paul Gosney

The placement of the large horseshoe-shaped bar is highlighted by the intensity of the tangerine beaded jelly-like chandeliers above. A screen device ensures a separate function area while remaining visually connected.

Totem Bar

CHO SLADE ARCHITECTURE WITH ANTHONY FONTENOT

The architects connected two separate storefronts and created a bar and restaurant/lounge, emphasizing the distinction between the two environments. The client was interested in totems and carved panels, exhibiting them prominently, and building spaces around them. In response, the architects decided that the idea for each room should come from ideas embedded in totems.

For the bar, the focus was on the object quality of totems, as freestanding objects in a landscape. The bar becomes the central focus of the space but each component has a strong separate quality. In the lounge, the architects wanted to explore the idea of carving itself, how a totem is carved out of one tree, one material. The entire space is a container defined by one material that unifies the wall, ceiling, seating, and tables. In contrast to the bar, this space is more like a cave carved out of felt.

Additionally, these spaces offer distinct experiences, with the bar more amenable to mixing and meeting while the restaurant/lounge is closer and fosters a relaxed, intimate setting.

Transport

MADDISON ARCHITECTS

Located in the hub of transportation, the trams, trains, pedestrians, and automobiles heavily impact on the venue's site. The positioning of the building within a large urban space (Federation Square) allowed for maximum permeability between the pub and the site.

The idea of the main entrance was de-formalized, with each door being presented as a back door. Inside, the form making dominates and dictates the spatiality and spatial interaction. The heavy forms create a continuous element that breaks, encloses, and delineates a notion of intimate spaces within a large volume. Within these nooks and crannies, the clientele are forced into introverted social groups, or they are pressed against the glass for extroverted exposure.

The juncture between hard and soft, and reflective and textured surfaces formalizes a robust language to suit the utilitarian nature of a pub. Elements expressed horizontally emphasize the large footprint and vertical elements used to express the height of the space.

Every element of Transport, including the display keg room, communal inbuilt seating, and leaning rails reinforces the notion of a modern-day pub. The space suggests the notion of 'pub' and embraces its context and site.

Photography: Rhiannon Slater

Universum Lounge

PLAJER & FRANZ STUDIO

The Universum lounge is located in what was once the largest movie theater in Berlin, a 1920's German landmark designed by Bauhaus pioneer Erich Mendelsohn. The client had initially requested the creation of an ice-cream parlor but the architects convinced the owner that the venue was too small for ice-cream counters; and that the neighborhood was lacking a bar.

For the architects, the name 'Universum' will always be connected with the most exciting event in space—the day man landed on the moon. From this they took their creative hook, fashioning an interior reminiscent of the loungerooms in which the world watched the event, broadcast from their teak television sets. The architecture is a further development of the dynamic and futuristic modernism of the 1950s and 1960s where Corbusier mixed concrete with wood. It is a South American modernism like that of Oscar Niemeyer's, linked to the present day by its visitors and the use of the materials and the machines that shaped the interior.

Vucciria

This geometric and symmetrical space was drafted and constructed by AE3 [Architects and Engineers]. Flux Design worked closely with Anne Kustner Lighting Design, to integrate virtually every interior fixture with intelligent LED lighting technologies.

By day, the interior is notably achromatic and crisp, characterized by bold contrasts in the tone and texture of the materials and finishes. By night, the entire space transforms into color. More than 200 independently programmable lighting units, capable of 16.7 million colors each, dissolve and pulsate throughout the space.

Specialty lighting elements were integrated into the lower-level bar surface and facing, back bar shelves and canopy structure, as well as the upper-level bar surface, back bar structure, and the entire mezzanine railing system. A thorough understanding of material properties and an innovative method of approaching them enable Flux Design to bridge the gap between designer and builder, without losing sight of the client's wants and needs.

Owners, Joe and Mimma Megna, along with interior designer Jon Schlagenhaft Design, are noted for their insistence on quality and impeccable attention to detail. Each fixture in Vucciria, hand crafted by Flux's team of artists and designers, was constructed from the very best materials, all the way down to the host station and stair rail.

Photography: courtesy Flux Design

White Bar

GRANT AMON ARCHITECTS PTY LTD

Set within the old George Hotel, a St Kilda landmark since the 1880s, the White Bar and Gallery is a new refit of an existing function room. The bar is centrally located between existing columns with ornate cornicing, and features a backlit circular red Marblo display unit that hovers like a setting sun. The red dot 'logo' is prominent from the streetscape at night, providing its own neon signage.

The room is predominantly white, including the bar, acknowledging its gallery function, while the deep reds of the bar top, display shelving, and wall carpeting provide a lush contrast. The entire rear wall has retractable sheer metallic curtains that allow art to be displayed. New George Nelson pendant lights hover over the flexible area that operates as a function room, late-night bar, or gallery space. A separate smaller room is also available for functions or simply an extra lounge area and is notable for its random red tones of striped floor and wall carpet lining.

Photography: Trevor Mein

York Event Theatre

II BY IV DESIGN ASSOCIATES INC.

Illumination plays an important role in the exterior and interior aspects of II BY IV's elegant and modish concept for the York renovation. It starts with the use of fiber optics, illuminated signage boxes, and a large video board to add color, light, and movement to the theater's existing monolithic concrete slab face, creating a striking and beacon-like street presence. The large lobby sparkles with white stone flooring, metal wall paneling, illuminated displays filled with glass sculptures, and custom glass drop chandeliers.

Throughout the facility the architects placed illuminated bar features, mirrored walls, ceilings, and display niches, creating a stunning play of light and shadow on unique wood block wall features. Graceful custom furnishings and a palette of taupes and reds add warmth and comfort.

Party organizers find the York Event Theatre an already 'fully dressed' facility that will demand no additional décor items beyond floral arrangements and the party-goers' own clothing and jewelry. Distinctive, vibrant, and chic, the York Event Theatre will accommodate cocktails for single groups as large as 1800, full banquet service for 800, or smaller combinations across three floors.

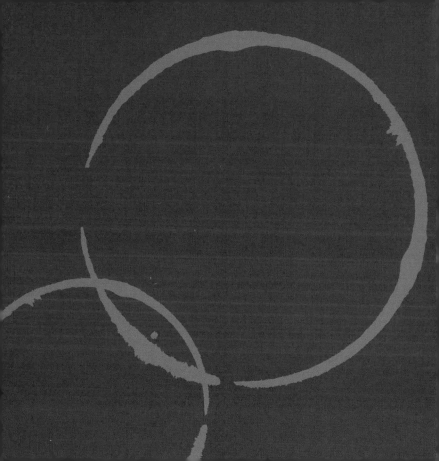

INDEX

Index of Architects